NATIONAL PARKS
BUCKET JOURNAL

NATIONAL PARKS IN ALPHABETICAL ORDER

A

Acadia

American Samoa

Arches

B

Badlands

Big Bend

Biscayne

Black Canyon of the Gunnison

Bryce Canyon

C

Canyonlands

Capitol Reef

Carlsbad Caverns

Channel Islands

Congaree

Crater Lake

Cuyahoga Valley

D

Death Valley

Denali

Dry Tortugas

E

Everglades

G

Gates of the Arctic

Gateway Arch

Glacier

Glacier Bay

Grand Canyon

Grand Teton

Great Basin

Great Sand Dunes

Great Smoky Mountains

Guadalupe Mountains

H

Haleakalā

Hawai'i Volcanoes

Hot Springs

I

Indiana Dunes

Isle Royale

J

Joshua Tree

K

Katmai

Kenai Fjords

Kings Canyon

Kobuk Valley

L

Lake Clark

Lassen Volcanic

M

Mammoth Cave

Mesa Verde

Mount Rainier

N

New River Gorge

North Cascades

O

Olympic

P

Petrified Forest

Pinnacles

R

Redwood

Rocky Mountain

S

Saguaro

Sequoia

Shenandoah

T

Theodore Roosevelt

V

Virgin Islands

Voyageurs

W

White Sands

Wind Cave

Wrangell–St. Elias

Y

Yellowstone

Yosemite

Z

Zion

MY BUCKET LIST

No.	Park Name	Date
1		
2		
3		
4		
5		
6		
7		
8		
9		
10		
11		
12		
13		
14		
15		
16		
17		
18		
19		
20		

21		
22		
23		
24		
25		
26		
27		
28		
29		
30		
31		
32		
33		
34		
35		
36		
37		
38		
39		
40		
41		
42		
43		

44		
45		
46		
47		
48		
49		
50		
51		
52		
53		
54		
55		
56		
57		
58		
59		
60		
61		
62		
63		

TRACKING LOG

Alaska

National Park	Order	Visited
Denali		
Gates of the Arctic		
Glacier Bay		
Katmai		
Kenai Fjords		
Kobuk Valley		
Lake Clark		
Wrangell-St. Elias		

American Samoa

National Park	Order	Visited
National Park of American Samoa		

Arizona

National Park	Order	Visited
Grand Canyon		
Petrified Forest		
Saguaro		

Arkansas

National Park	Order	Visited
Hot Springs		

California

National Park	Order	Visited
Channel Islands		
Death Valley		
Joshua Tree		
Kings Canyon		
Lassen Volcanic		
Pinnacles		
Redwood		
Sequoia		
Yosemite National Park		

California

National Park	Order	Visited
Black Canyon of the Gunnison		
Great Sand Dunes		
Mesa Verde		
Rocky Mountain		

Florida

National Park	Order	Visited
Biscayne		
Dry Tortugas		
Everglades		

Hawaii

National Park	Order	Visited
Haleakala		
Hawai'i Volcanoes		

Idaho, Montana & Wyoming

National Park	Order	Visited
Yellowstone		

Kentucky

National Park	Order	Visited
Mammoth Cave		

Indiana

National Park	Order	Visited
Indiana Dunes		

Maine

National Park	Order	Visited
Acadia		

Michigan

National Park	Order	Visited
Isle Royale		

Minnesota

National Park	Order	Visited
Voyageurs		

Missouri

National Park	Order	Visited
Gateway Arch		

Montana

National Park	Order	Visited
Glacier		
Yellowstone		

Nevada

National Park	Order	Visited
Death Valley		
Great Basin		

New Mexico

National Park	Order	Visited
Carlsbad Caverns		
White Sands		

North Dakota

National Park	Order	Visited
Theodore Roosevelt National Park		

North Carolina & Tennessee

National Park	Order	Visited
Great Smoky Mountains		

Ohio

National Park	Order	Visited
Cuyahoga Valley		

Oregon

National Park	Order	Visited
Crater Lake		

South Carolina

National Park	Order	Visited
Congaree		

South Dakota

National Park	Order	Visited
Badlands		
Wind Cave		

Texas

National Park	Order	Visited
Big Bend		
Guadalupe Mountains		

Utah

National Park	Order	Visited
Arches		
Bryce Canyon		
Canyonlands		
Capitol Reef		
Zion		

Virgin Islands

National Park	Order	Visited
Virgin Islands		

Virgina

National Park	Order	Visited
Shenandoah		

Washington

National Park	Order	Visited
Mount Rainier		
North Cascades		
Olympic		

West Virgina

National Park	Order	Visited
New River Gorge		

Wyoming

National Park	Order	
Grand Teton		
Yellowstone		

STORAGE

Equipment

Current State	Necessary State	Where to get/buy/learn

Skills

Current State	Necessary State	Where to get/buy/learn

Condition

Current State	Necessary State	Where to get/buy/learn

Knowledge

Current State	Necessary State	Where to get/buy/learn

Knowledge the area I'm going to

Current State	Necessary State	Where to get/buy/learn

ACADIA
NATIONAL PARK

DATE: / /   **FEE:**

TEMP:

Who was with me	Where I stayed

Sights I took in	Wildlife I saw

Rating	# of days visited
☆☆☆☆☆☆☆☆☆☆	1 2 3 4 5 6 7+

Popular attractions I visited/experienced

☐ Cadillac Mountain   ☐ Schoodic Point

☐ Jordan Pond   ☐ Thunder Hole

☐ Sand Beach   ☐

☐ Park Loop Road   ☐

My Favorite moment

Place for your stamp and overall experience

American Samoa
NATIONAL PARK

DATE: / /   FEE:

TEMP:

Who was with me	Where I stayed

Sights I took in	Wildlife I saw

Rating	# of days visited
☆☆☆☆☆☆☆☆☆☆	1 2 3 4 5 6 7+

Popular attractions I visited/experienced

- [ ] National Park of American Samoa
- [ ] Two Dollar Beach
- [ ] Mount Alava
- [ ] Lower Sauma Ridge Hike
- [ ] Ofu Beach
- [ ] Tauese P.F. Sunia Ocean Center
- [ ]
- [ ]

My Favorite moment

Place for your stamp and overall experience

Arches
NATIONAL PARK

DATE: /   /   FEE:

TEMP:

Who was with me	Where I stayed

Sights I took in	Wildlife I saw

Rating	# of days visited
☆☆☆☆☆☆☆☆☆☆	1 2 3 4 5 6 7+

Popular attractions I visited/experienced

☐ Delicate Arch Hike   ☐ Fiery Furnace Overlook and Hike

☐ Windows Section   ☐ Devil's Garden Hike and Landscape Arch

☐ Double Arch   ☐

☐ Park Avenue Hike   ☐

My Favorite moment

Place for your stamp and overall experience

Badlands
NATIONAL PARK

DATE: /   /   FEE:

TEMP:

Who was with me	Where I stayed

Sights I took in	Wildlife I saw

Rating	# of days visited
☆☆☆☆☆☆☆☆☆☆	1 2 3 4 5 6 7+

Popular attractions I visited/experienced

☐ Loop Road   ☐ Roberts Prairie Dog Town

☐ Badlands Wall   ☐ Big Badlands Overlook

☐ Notch Trail   ☐

☐ Yellow Mounds Overlook   ☐

My Favorite moment

Place for your stamp and overall experience

Big Bend
NATIONAL PARK

DATE: / /   **FEE:**

TEMP:

Who was with me	Where I stayed

Sights I took in	Wildlife I saw

Rating	# of days visited
☆☆☆☆☆☆☆☆☆☆	1 2 3 4 5 6 7+

Popular attractions I visited/experienced

☐ Closed Canyon   ☐ Dog Canyon

☐ The South Rim Loop   ☐ Santa Elena Canyon

☐ The Window Trail   ☐

☐ Boquillas Canyon   ☐

My Favorite moment

Place for your stamp and overall experience

Biscayne
NATIONAL PARK

DATE: /   /   FEE:

☀ ⛅ ☁ 🌦 🌧 ⛈ 🌨 🌨   TEMP:

Who was with me	Where I stayed

Sights I took in	Wildlife I saw

Rating	# of days visited
☆☆☆☆☆☆☆☆☆☆	1 2 3 4 5 6 7+

Popular attractions I visited/experienced

☐ Bill Baggs Cape Florida State Park   ☐ Crandon Park

☐ Crandon Golf Course   ☐ Key Biscayne Village Green Park.

☐ Ayesha Saffron   ☐

☐ Stiltsville   ☐

My Favorite moment

Place for your stamp and overall experience

Black Canyon of the Gunnison
NATIONAL PARK

DATE: / /   **FEE:**

TEMP:

Who was with me	Where I stayed

Sights I took in	Wildlife I saw

Rating	# of days visited
☆☆☆☆☆☆☆☆☆☆	1 2 3 4 5 6 7+

Popular attractions I visited/experienced

- ☐ South Rim Road
- ☐ Warner Point
- ☐ North Rim
- ☐ Painted Wall

- ☐ East Portal Road
- ☐ Rim Rock Trail
- ☐
- ☐

My Favorite moment

Place for your stamp and overall experience

Bryce Canyon
NATIONAL PARK

DATE: / /   **FEE:**

TEMP:

Who was with me	Where I stayed

Sights I took in	Wildlife I saw

Rating	# of days visited
☆☆☆☆☆☆☆☆☆☆	1 2 3 4 5 6 7+

Popular attractions I visited/experienced

☐ Sunset Point   ☐ Rainbow Point

☐ Inspiration Point   ☐ Queens Garden Loop

☐ Thor's Hammer   ☐

☐ Bryce Amphitheatre   ☐

My Favorite moment

Place for your stamp and overall experience

Canyonlands
NATIONAL PARK

DATE: / /   FEE:

TEMP:

Who was with me	Where I stayed

Sights I took in	Wildlife I saw

Rating	# of days visited
☆☆☆☆☆☆☆☆☆☆	1 2 3 4 5 6 7+

Popular attractions I visited/experienced

- [ ] Mesa Arch
- [ ] Island in the Sky
- [ ] Grand View Point Overlook
- [ ] Shafer Trail

- [ ] The Needles
- [ ] Dead Horse Point State Park
- [ ]
- [ ]

My Favorite moment

Place for your stamp and overall experience

Capitol Reef
NATIONAL PARK

DATE: /   /   FEE:

TEMP:

Who was with me	Where I stayed

Sights I took in	Wildlife I saw

Rating	# of days visited
☆☆☆☆☆☆☆☆☆☆	1 2 3 4 5 6 7+

Popular attractions I visited/experienced

- [ ] The Hickman Bridge Trail
- [ ] Burr Trail
- [ ] Cassidy Arch
- [ ] Fruita
- [ ] Capitol Gorge Trail
- [ ] Fremont Petroglyphs
- [ ]
- [ ]

My Favorite moment

Place for your stamp and overall experience

Carlsbad Caverns
NATIONAL PARK

DATE: / / **FEE:**

TEMP:

Who was with me	Where I stayed

Sights I took in	Wildlife I saw

Rating	# of days visited
☆☆☆☆☆☆☆☆☆☆	1 2 3 4 5 6 7+

Popular attractions I visited/experienced

- [ ] Lion's Tail
- [ ] Bat Flight Program
- [ ] King's Palace
- [ ] Big Room

- [ ] Giant Dome
- [ ] Bottomless Pit
- [ ]
- [ ]

My Favorite moment

Place for your stamp and overall experience

Channel Islands
NATIONAL PARK

DATE: / / **FEE:**

☀ ⛅ ☁ 🌧 🌦 ⛈ 🌨 🌨 **TEMP:**

Who was with me	Where I stayed

Sights I took in	Wildlife I saw

Rating	# of days visited
☆☆☆☆☆☆☆☆☆☆	1 2 3 4 5 6 7+

Popular attractions I visited/experienced

- [ ] The Sea Caves
- [ ] Channel Islands National Marine Sanctuary
- [ ] Santa Barbara Island
- [ ] San Miguel Island
- [ ] Anacapa Island
- [ ] Santa Cruz Island
- [ ]
- [ ]

My Favorite moment

Place for your stamp and overall experience

Congaree
NATIONAL PARK

DATE: / /   **FEE:**

☀ ⛅ ☁ 🌦 🌧 ⛈ 🌨 ❄   **TEMP:**

Who was with me	Where I stayed

Sights I took in	Wildlife I saw

Rating	# of days visited
☆☆☆☆☆☆☆☆☆☆	1 2 3 4 5 6 7+

Popular attractions I visited/experienced

☐ Hiking a Trail ☐ Camping

☐ Canoeing and Kayaking ☐ Fishing

☐ Ranger Led Canoe Tour ☐

☐ Catch the synchronous Fireflies ☐

My Favorite moment

Place for your stamp and overall experience

Crater Lake
NATIONAL PARK

DATE: / /   FEE:

TEMP:

Who was with me	Where I stayed

Sights I took in	Wildlife I saw

Rating	# of days visited
☆☆☆☆☆☆☆☆☆☆	1 2 3 4 5 6 7+

Popular attractions I visited/experienced

- [ ] Rim Drive
- [ ] Crater Lake
- [ ] Cleetwood Cove Trail
- [ ] Toketee Falls
- [ ] Wizard Island
- [ ] Pinnacles Overlook Hike
- [ ]
- [ ]

My Favorite moment

Place for your stamp and overall experience

Cuyahoga Valley
NATIONAL PARK

DATE: / /   **FEE:**

TEMP:

Who was with me	Where I stayed

Sights I took in	Wildlife I saw

Rating	# of days visited
☆☆☆☆☆☆☆☆☆☆	1 2 3 4 5 6 7+

Popular attractions I visited/experienced

- ☐ Beaver Marsh
- ☐ Boston Mill Visitor Center
- ☐ Brandywine Falls
- ☐ Canal Exploration Center

- ☐ Frazee House
- ☐ Ritchie Ledges
- ☐
- ☐

My Favorite moment

Place for your stamp and overall experience

Death Valley
NATIONAL PARK

DATE: /   /   FEE:

TEMP:

Who was with me	Where I stayed

Sights I took in	Wildlife I saw

Rating	# of days visited
☆☆☆☆☆☆☆☆☆☆	1 2 3 4 5 6 7+

Popular attractions I visited/experienced

☐ Wildrose Charcoal Kilns   ☐ Ubehebe Crater

☐ Mosaic Canyon   ☐ Racetrack Playa

☐ Devils Golf Course   ☐

☐ Artists Palette   ☐

My Favorite moment

Place for your stamp and overall experience

Denali
NATIONAL PARK

DATE: / / **FEE:**

☀ ⛅ ☁ 🌧 🌧 ⛈ 🌧 🌨 **TEMP:**

Who was with me	Where I stayed

Sights I took in	Wildlife I saw

Rating	# of days visited
☆☆☆☆☆☆☆☆☆☆	1 2 3 4 5 6 7+

Popular attractions I visited/experienced

☐ Husky Homestead   ☐ Mt. Healy Overlook Trail

☐ Park Road   ☐ Savage Alpine Trail

☐ Horseshoe Lake Trail   ☐

☐ Wonder Lake   ☐

My Favorite moment

Place for your stamp and overall experience

Dry Tortugas
NATIONAL PARK

DATE: / /   **FEE:**

TEMP:

Who was with me	Where I stayed

Sights I took in	Wildlife I saw

Rating	# of days visited
☆☆☆☆☆☆☆☆☆☆	1 2 3 4 5 6 7+

Popular attractions I visited/experienced

- ☐ Fort Jefferson   ☐
- ☐ Garden Key   ☐
- ☐ Little Africa   ☐
- ☐ Tortugas Banks   ☐

My Favorite moment

Place for your stamp and overall experience

Everglades
NATIONAL PARK

DATE: / /   **FEE:**

TEMP:

Who was with me	Where I stayed

Sights I took in	Wildlife I saw

Rating	# of days visited
☆☆☆☆☆☆☆☆☆☆	1 2 3 4 5 6 7+

Popular attractions I visited/experienced

☐ Shark Valley   ☐ Flamingo

☐ Anhinga Trail   ☐ Mahogany Hammock

☐ Ernest F. Coe Visitor Center   ☐

☐ Nine Mile Pond Canoe Trail   ☐

My Favorite moment

Place for your stamp and overall experience

Gates of the Arctic
NATIONAL PARK

DATE: / /   **FEE:**

TEMP:

Who was with me	Where I stayed

Sights I took in	Wildlife I saw

Rating	# of days visited
☆☆☆☆☆☆☆☆☆☆	1 2 3 4 5 6 7+

Popular attractions I visited/experienced

☐ Koyukuk River   ☐ Kugururok River

☐ Kobuk Wild River   ☐ Tinayguk River

☐ John River   ☐

☐ Boreal Mountain   ☐

My Favorite moment

Place for your stamp and overall experience

Gateway Arch
NATIONAL PARK

DATE: / /   **FEE:**

TEMP:

Who was with me	Where I stayed

Sights I took in	Wildlife I saw

Rating	# of days visited
☆☆☆☆☆☆☆☆☆☆	1 2 3 4 5 6 7+

Popular attractions I visited/experienced

- [ ] Tram Ride to the Top.
- [ ] Helicopter Tours
- [ ] The Museum at the Gateway Arch
- [ ]
- [ ] Riverboat Cruises
- [ ]
- [ ] Old Courthouse
- [ ]

My Favorite moment

Place for your stamp and overall experience

Glacier
NATIONAL PARK

DATE: / / FEE:

TEMP:

Who was with me	Where I stayed

Sights I took in	Wildlife I saw

Rating	# of days visited
☆☆☆☆☆☆☆☆☆☆	1 2 3 4 5 6 7+

Popular attractions I visited/experienced

☐ Going-to-the-Sun Road   ☐ Highline Trail

☐ Grinnell Glacier   ☐ Logan Pass

☐ Lake McDonald   ☐

☐ Avalanche Lake   ☐

My Favorite moment

Place for your stamp and overall experience

Glacier Bay
NATIONAL PARK

DATE: / /   **FEE:**

TEMP:

Who was with me	Where I stayed

Sights I took in	Wildlife I saw

Rating	# of days visited
☆☆☆☆☆☆☆☆☆☆	1 2 3 4 5 6 7+

Popular attractions I visited/experienced

- ☐ Flying over Glacier Bay
- ☐ Glacier Bay Boat Tour
- ☐ Taz Whale Watching Tour
- ☐ Sunset at Halibut Point
- ☐ Hiking in the rain forest
- ☐ Exploring the coast at low tide
- ☐
- ☐

My Favorite moment

Place for your stamp and overall experience

Grand Canyon
NATIONAL PARK

DATE: /   /   **FEE:**

TEMP:

Who was with me	Where I stayed

Sights I took in	Wildlife I saw

Rating	# of days visited
☆☆☆☆☆☆☆☆☆☆	1 2 3 4 5 6 7+

Popular attractions I visited/experienced

☐ Grand Canyon South Rim   ☐ Rim Trail

☐ Bright Angel Trail   ☐ Mather Point

☐ Grand Canyon North Rim   ☐

☐ South Kaibab Trail   ☐

My Favorite moment

Place for your stamp and overall experience

Grand Teton
NATIONAL PARK

DATE: / /   **FEE:**

☀ ⛅ ☁ 🌧 🌧 ⛈ 🌨 ❄   **TEMP:**

Who was with me	Where I stayed

Sights I took in	Wildlife I saw

Rating	# of days visited
☆☆☆☆☆☆☆☆☆☆	1 2 3 4 5 6 7+

Popular attractions I visited/experienced

- ☐ Jenny Lake Trail
- ☐ 42-mile Scenic Loop Drive
- ☐ Chapel of the Transfiguration
- ☐ Moose Wilson Road

- ☐ Snake River Overlook
- ☐ Jackson Lake
- ☐
- ☐

My Favorite moment

Place for your stamp and overall experience

Great Basin
NATIONAL PARK

DATE: /   /   FEE:

TEMP:

Who was with me	Where I stayed

Sights I took in	Wildlife I saw

Rating	# of days visited
☆☆☆☆☆☆☆☆☆☆	1 2 3 4 5 6 7+

Popular attractions I visited/experienced

- [ ] Lehman Caves
- [ ] Wheeler Peak
- [ ] Bristlecone Trails
- [ ] Alpine Lakes Loop
- [ ] Teresa Lake
- [ ] Stella Lake
- [ ]
- [ ]

My Favorite moment

Place for your stamp and overall experience

Great Sand Dunes
NATIONAL PARK

DATE: / /   **FEE:**

TEMP:

Who was with me	Where I stayed

Sights I took in	Wildlife I saw

Rating	# of days visited
☆☆☆☆☆☆☆☆☆☆	1 2 3 4 5 6 7+

Popular attractions I visited/experienced

☐ High Dune Trail   ☐ Mosca Pass Trail

☐ Little Medano Creek   ☐ Montville Nature Trail

☐ Mosca Pass Trail   ☐

☐ Mosca Pass Trail   ☐

My Favorite moment

Place for your stamp and overall experience

Great Smoky Mountains
NATIONAL PARK

DATE: / /   **FEE:**

TEMP:

Who was with me	Where I stayed

Sights I took in	Wildlife I saw

Rating	# of days visited
☆☆☆☆☆☆☆☆☆☆	1 2 3 4 5 6 7+

Popular attractions I visited/experienced

- [ ] Roaring Fork Motor Nature Trail
- [ ] Laurel Falls
- [ ] Foothills Parkway
- [ ] Chimneys Picnic Area
- [ ] Clingmans Dome
- [ ]
- [ ] Cades Cove
- [ ]

My Favorite moment

Place for your stamp and overall experience

Guadalupe Mountains
NATIONAL PARK

DATE: / /   **FEE:**

TEMP:

Who was with me	Where I stayed

Sights I took in	Wildlife I saw

Rating	# of days visited
☆☆☆☆☆☆☆☆☆☆	1 2 3 4 5 6 7+

Popular attractions I visited/experienced

☐ McKittrick Canyon   ☐ Pratt Cabin

☐ Devil's Hall Trail   ☐ Permian Reef Geology Trail

☐ El Capitan   ☐

☐ Dog Canyon   ☐

My Favorite moment

Place for your stamp and overall experience

Haleakalā
NATIONAL PARK

DATE: /   /   **FEE:**

☀ ⛅ ☁ 🌦 🌧 ⛈ 🌨 🌨   **TEMP:**

Who was with me	Where I stayed
Sights I took in	Wildlife I saw
Rating	# of days visited
☆☆☆☆☆☆☆☆☆☆	1 2 3 4 5 6 7+

Popular attractions I visited/experienced

☐ Haleakala Crater   ☐ Haleakala Sunrise Tours

☐ Pipiwai Trail   ☐ Haleakala Observatories

☐ Supply Trail   ☐

☐ Ohe'o Gulch   ☐

My Favorite moment

Place for your stamp and overall experience

Hawai'i Volcanoes
NATIONAL PARK

DATE: /   /   FEE:

TEMP:

Who was with me	Where I stayed

Sights I took in	Wildlife I saw

Rating	# of days visited
☆☆☆☆☆☆☆☆☆☆	1 2 3 4 5 6 7+

Popular attractions I visited/experienced

☐ Kilauea Iki Trail   ☐ Kalapana

☐ Kilauea Iki Trail   ☐ Sulphur Banks

☐ Nahuku - Thurston Lava Tube   ☐

☐ Holei Sea Arch   ☐

My Favorite moment

Place for your stamp and overall experience

Hot Springs
NATIONAL PARK

DATE: /   /   FEE:

TEMP:

Who was with me	Where I stayed

Sights I took in	Wildlife I saw

Rating	# of days visited
☆☆☆☆☆☆☆☆☆☆	1 2 3 4 5 6 7+

Popular attractions I visited/experienced

- ☐ Garvan Woodland Gardens
- ☐ Bathhouse Row
- ☐ Fordyce Bathhouse
- ☐ Lake Catherine State Park
- ☐ Mid-America Science Museum
- ☐ Anthony Chapel
- ☐
- ☐

My Favorite moment

Place for your stamp and overall experience

Indiana Dunes
NATIONAL PARK

DATE: / / **FEE:**

TEMP:

Who was with me	Where I stayed

Sights I took in	Wildlife I saw

Rating	# of days visited
☆☆☆☆☆☆☆☆☆☆	1 2 3 4 5 6 7+

Popular attractions I visited/experienced

- [ ] Taltree Arboretum and Gardens
- [ ] Chapel of the Resurrection
- [ ] Portage Lakefront and Riverwalk
- [ ] Ogden Dunes Beach
- [ ] Cowles Bog
- [ ] Coffee Creek Watershed Preserve
- [ ]
- [ ]

My Favorite moment

Place for your stamp and overall experience

Isle Royale
NATIONAL PARK

DATE: / /　　　　　**FEE:**

TEMP:

Who was with me	Where I stayed

Sights I took in	Wildlife I saw

Rating	# of days visited
☆☆☆☆☆☆☆☆☆☆	1　2　3　4　5　6　7+

Popular attractions I visited/experienced

☐ Scoville Point　　　　　☐

☐ Rock Harbor　　　　　☐

☐ Rock Island Lighthouse　☐

☐ Lookout Louise　　　　☐

My Favorite moment

Place for your stamp and overall experience

Joshua Tree
NATIONAL PARK

DATE: / /   **FEE:**

TEMP:

Who was with me	Where I stayed

Sights I took in	Wildlife I saw

Rating	# of days visited
☆☆☆☆☆☆☆☆☆☆	1 2 3 4 5 6 7+

Popular attractions I visited/experienced

- ☐ Hidden Valley
- ☐ Cholla Cactus Garden
- ☐ Keys View
- ☐ Barker Dam Trail
- ☐ Ryan Mountain
- ☐ Arch Rock
- ☐
- ☐

My Favorite moment

Place for your stamp and overall experience

Katmai
NATIONAL PARK

DATE: / /   **FEE:**

TEMP:

Who was with me	Where I stayed

Sights I took in	Wildlife I saw

Rating	# of days visited
☆☆☆☆☆☆☆☆☆☆	1 2 3 4 5 6 7+

Popular attractions I visited/experienced

☐ Brooks Falls

☐ Brooks River

☐ Valley of Ten Thousand Smokes

☐ Naknek Lake

☐ Savonoski Loop

☐ Baked Mountain

☐

☐

My Favorite moment

Place for your stamp and overall experience

Kenai Fjords
NATIONAL PARK

DATE: / / **FEE:**

TEMP:

Who was with me	Where I stayed

Sights I took in	Wildlife I saw

Rating	# of days visited
☆☆☆☆☆☆☆☆☆☆	1 2 3 4 5 6 7+

Popular attractions I visited/experienced

☐ Exit Glacier ☐ Pederson Glacier

☐ Harding Ice Field Trail ☐ Clam Gulch

☐ Fox Island ☐

☐ Six Mile Creek ☐

My Favorite moment

Place for your stamp and overall experience

Kings Canyon
NATIONAL PARK

DATE: / /   **FEE:**

TEMP:

Who was with me	Where I stayed

Sights I took in	Wildlife I saw

Rating	# of days visited
☆☆☆☆☆☆☆☆☆☆	1 2 3 4 5 6 7+

Popular attractions I visited/experienced

- [ ] Buck Rock Lookout
- [ ] Giant Forest
- [ ] Moro Rock Trail
- [ ] Kings Canyon

- [ ] Crescent Meadow Loop
- [ ] Generals Highway
- [ ]
- [ ]

My Favorite moment

Place for your stamp and overall experience

Kobuk Valley
NATIONAL PARK

DATE: /   /   **FEE:**

TEMP:

Who was with me	Where I stayed
Sights I took in	**Wildlife I saw**

Rating	# of days visited
☆☆☆☆☆☆☆☆☆☆	1 2 3 4 5 6 7+

Popular attractions I visited/experienced

☐ Boating   ☐ Skiing

☐ Hiking   ☐ Snow machining

☐ Wildlife watching   ☐

☐ Dog mushing   ☐

My Favorite moment

Place for your stamp and overall experience

Lake Clark
NATIONAL PARK

DATE: /   /   **FEE:**

TEMP:

Who was with me	Where I stayed

Sights I took in	Wildlife I saw

Rating	# of days visited
☆☆☆☆☆☆☆☆☆☆	1 2 3 4 5 6 7+

Popular attractions I visited/experienced

- [ ] Turquoise Lake
- [ ] Mulchatna River
- [ ] Chilikadrotna River
- [ ] Turquoise Valley

- [ ]
- [ ]
- [ ]
- [ ]

My Favorite moment

Place for your stamp and overall experience

Lassen Volcanic
NATIONAL PARK

DATE: /   /   FEE:

TEMP:

Who was with me	Where I stayed

Sights I took in	Wildlife I saw

Rating	# of days visited
☆☆☆☆☆☆☆☆☆☆	1 2 3 4 5 6 7+

Popular attractions I visited/experienced

- [ ] Mount Lassen
- [ ] Manzanita Lake
- [ ] Bumpass Hell
- [ ] Sulphur Works

- [ ] Cinder Cone
- [ ] Kings Creek Falls
- [ ]
- [ ]

My Favorite moment

Place for your stamp and overall experience

Mammoth Cave
NATIONAL PARK

DATE: / /   **FEE:**

☀ ⛅ ☁ 🌦 🌧 ⛈ 🌧 🌨   **TEMP:**

Who was with me	Where I stayed

Sights I took in	Wildlife I saw

Rating	# of days visited
☆☆☆☆☆☆☆☆☆☆	1 2 3 4 5 6 7+

Popular attractions I visited/experienced

☐ Fat Man's Misery   ☐ Echo River

☐ Mammoth Cave   ☐ Tall Man's Misery

☐ Cedar Sink Trail   ☐

☐ Green River   ☐

My Favorite moment

Place for your stamp and overall experience

Mesa Verde
NATIONAL PARK

DATE: /   /   FEE:

TEMP:

Who was with me	Where I stayed

Sights I took in	Wildlife I saw

Rating	# of days visited
☆☆☆☆☆☆☆☆☆☆	1 2 3 4 5 6 7+

Popular attractions I visited/experienced

☐ Cliff Palace   ☐ Spruce Tree House

☐ Balcony House   ☐ Ruins Road

☐ Long House   ☐

☐ Petroglyph Point Hike   ☐

My Favorite moment

Place for your stamp and overall experience

Mount Rainier
NATIONAL PARK

DATE: / /   **FEE:**

TEMP:

Who was with me	Where I stayed

Sights I took in	Wildlife I saw

Rating	# of days visited
☆☆☆☆☆☆☆☆☆☆	1 2 3 4 5 6 7+

Popular attractions I visited/experienced

☐ Skyline Trail   ☐ Narada Falls

☐ Grove of the Patriarchs   ☐ Christine Falls Viewpoint

☐ Tipsoo Lake Loop   ☐

☐ Paradise Valley   ☐

My Favorite moment

Place for your stamp and overall experience

New River Gorge
NATIONAL PARK

DATE: / /	FEE:

 TEMP:

Who was with me	Where I stayed

Sights I took in	Wildlife I saw

Rating	# of days visited
☆☆☆☆☆☆☆☆☆☆	1 2 3 4 5 6 7+

Popular attractions I visited/experienced

☐ New River Gorge Bridge   ☐ Thurmond

☐ Sandstone Falls   ☐ Glade Creek / Hamlet

☐ Nuttallburg   ☐

☐ Fayette Station Road   ☐

My Favorite moment

Place for your stamp and overall experience

North Cascades
NATIONAL PARK

DATE: / /   **FEE:**

TEMP:

Who was with me	Where I stayed

Sights I took in	Wildlife I saw

Rating	# of days visited
☆☆☆☆☆☆☆☆☆☆	1 2 3 4 5 6 7+

Popular attractions I visited/experienced

☐ North Cascades Highway

☐ Diablo Lake Overlook

☐ Washington Pass Overlook

☐ Maple Pass Loop

☐ Ross Lake National Recreation Area

☐ Cascade Pass

☐

☐

My Favorite moment

Place for your stamp and overall experience

Olympic
NATIONAL PARK

DATE: / /   **FEE:**

TEMP:

Who was with me	Where I stayed

Sights I took in	Wildlife I saw

Rating	# of days visited
☆☆☆☆☆☆☆☆☆☆	1 2 3 4 5 6 7+

Popular attractions I visited/experienced

☐ Ruby Beach   ☐ Sol Duc Falls

☐ Hoh Rain Forest   ☐ Hurricane Ridge

☐ Olympic National Forest   ☐

☐ Rialto Beach   ☐

My Favorite moment

Place for your stamp and overall experience

Petrified Forest
NATIONAL PARK

DATE: /   /   **FEE:**

TEMP:

Who was with me	Where I stayed

Sights I took in	Wildlife I saw

Rating	# of days visited
☆☆☆☆☆☆☆☆☆☆	1 2 3 4 5 6 7+

Popular attractions I visited/experienced

- ☐ Painted Desert
- ☐ Blue Mesa
- ☐ Crystal Forest Trail
- ☐ Rainbow Forest

- ☐ Giant Logs Loop
- ☐ Jasper Forest
- ☐
- ☐

My Favorite moment

Place for your stamp and overall experience

Pinnacles
NATIONAL PARK

DATE: / / **FEE:**

☀ ⛅ ☁ 🌦 🌧 ⛈ 🌨 ❄ **TEMP:**

Who was with me	Where I stayed

Sights I took in	Wildlife I saw

Rating	# of days visited
☆☆☆☆☆☆☆☆☆☆	1 2 3 4 5 6 7+

Popular attractions I visited/experienced

☐ Talus Caves   ☐

☐ Bird Watching   ☐

☐ Rock Climbing   ☐

☐ Hiking Trails   ☐

My Favorite moment

Place for your stamp and overall experience

Redwood
NATIONAL PARK

DATE: / /   **FEE:**

TEMP:

Who was with me	Where I stayed

Sights I took in	Wildlife I saw

Rating	# of days visited
☆☆☆☆☆☆☆☆☆☆	1 2 3 4 5 6 7+

Popular attractions I visited/experienced

☐ Tall Trees Grove   ☐

☐ California Coastal Trail   ☐

☐ California Coastal Trail   ☐

☐ Little Bald Hill Trail   ☐

My Favorite moment

Place for your stamp and overall experience

Rocky Mountain
NATIONAL PARK

DATE: /   /   **FEE:**

TEMP:

Who was with me	Where I stayed

Sights I took in	Wildlife I saw

Rating	# of days visited
☆☆☆☆☆☆☆☆☆☆	1 2 3 4 5 6 7+

Popular attractions I visited/experienced

☐ Trail Ridge Road   ☐ Alberta Falls

☐ Emerald Lake Trail   ☐ Chapel on the Rock

☐ Bear Lake   ☐

☐ Old Fall River Road   ☐

My Favorite moment

Place for your stamp and overall experience

Saguaro
NATIONAL PARK

DATE: / /   **FEE:**

TEMP:

Who was with me	Where I stayed

Sights I took in	Wildlife I saw

Rating	# of days visited
☆☆☆☆☆☆☆☆☆☆	1 2 3 4 5 6 7+

Popular attractions I visited/experienced

☐ Valley View Overlook   ☐ Hike in Saguaro East

☐ Signal Hill Petroglyphs   ☐ Hike to Wassen Peak

☐ Desert Discovery Nature Trail   ☐

☐ Cactus Forest Drive   ☐

My Favorite moment

Place for your stamp and overall experience

Sequoia
NATIONAL PARK

DATE: / /   **FEE:**

☀ ⛅ ☁ 🌧 🌧 ⛈ 🌧 🌨   **TEMP:**

Who was with me	Where I stayed

Sights I took in	Wildlife I saw

Rating	# of days visited
☆☆☆☆☆☆☆☆☆☆	1 2 3 4 5 6 7+

Popular attractions I visited/experienced

☐ Moro Rock Trail   ☐ Big Trees Trail

☐ Grant Grove   ☐ Grizzly Falls

☐ Crescent Meadow Loop   ☐

☐ Crystal Cave   ☐

My Favorite moment

Place for your stamp and overall experience

Shenandoah
NATIONAL PARK

DATE: / /   **FEE:**

TEMP:

Who was with me	Where I stayed

Sights I took in	Wildlife I saw

Rating	# of days visited
☆☆☆☆☆☆☆☆☆☆	1 2 3 4 5 6 7+

Popular attractions I visited/experienced

☐ Skyline Drive   ☐ Mary's Rock Summit Trail

☐ Old Rag Mountain Hike   ☐ Rose River Falls

☐ Dark Hollow Falls   ☐

☐ Hawksbill Mountain   ☐

My Favorite moment

Place for your stamp and overall experience

Theodore Roosevelt
NATIONAL PARK

DATE: / /   **FEE:**

☀ ⛅ ☁ 🌦 🌧 ⛈ 🌨 🌨   **TEMP:**

Who was with me	Where I stayed

Sights I took in	Wildlife I saw

Rating	# of days visited
☆☆☆☆☆☆☆☆☆☆	1 2 3 4 5 6 7+

Popular attractions I visited/experienced

☐ Peaceful Valley   ☐ Buckhorn Trail

☐ North Unit   ☐ Sperati Point Trail

☐ Petrified Forest Loop   ☐

☐ Oxbow Overlook   ☐

My Favorite moment

Place for your stamp and overall experience

Virgin Islands
NATIONAL PARK

DATE: / /   **FEE:**

TEMP:

Who was with me	Where I stayed

Sights I took in	Wildlife I saw

Rating	# of days visited
☆☆☆☆☆☆☆☆☆☆	1 2 3 4 5 6 7+

Popular attractions I visited/experienced

☐ Trunk Bay Beach   ☐ Reef Bay Trail

☐ Cinnamon Bay   ☐ Salt Pond Bay

☐ Waterlemon Cay   ☐

☐ Hawksnest Beach   ☐

My Favorite moment

Place for your stamp and overall experience

Voyageurs
NATIONAL PARK

DATE: / /   **FEE:**

☀ ⛅ ☁ 🌧 🌧 ⛈ 🌧 🌨   **TEMP:**

Who was with me	Where I stayed

Sights I took in	Wildlife I saw

Rating	# of days visited
☆☆☆☆☆☆☆☆☆☆	1 2 3 4 5 6 7+

Popular attractions I visited/experienced

☐ Rainy Lake   ☐ Namakan Island

☐ Kabetogama Peninsula   ☐ Sullivan Bay Trail

☐ Ellsworth Rock Gardens   ☐

☐ Crane Lake   ☐

My Favorite moment

Place for your stamp and overall experience

White Sands
NATIONAL PARK

DATE: /   /   FEE:

TEMP:

Who was with me	Where I stayed

Sights I took in	Wildlife I saw

Rating	# of days visited
☆☆☆☆☆☆☆☆☆☆	1 2 3 4 5 6 7+

Popular attractions I visited/experienced

☐ Backcountry Camping   ☐ Picnicking

☐ Driving Dunes Drive   ☐ TEST

☐ Horses and Other Pack Animals ☐

☐ Native Plant Garden Tour   ☐

My Favorite moment

Place for your stamp and overall experience

Wind Cave
NATIONAL PARK

DATE: /   /   **FEE:**

TEMP:

Who was with me	Where I stayed

Sights I took in	Wildlife I saw

Rating	# of days visited
☆☆☆☆☆☆☆☆☆☆	1 2 3 4 5 6 7+

Popular attractions I visited/experienced

- ☐ Rankin Ridge Nature Trail   ☐
- ☐ Elk Mountain Nature Trail   ☐
- ☐ Wind Cave Canyon Trail   ☐
- ☐ Candlelight Cave Tour   ☐

My Favorite moment

Place for your stamp and overall experience

Wrangell–St. Elias
NATIONAL PARK

DATE: / /   **FEE:**

TEMP:

Who was with me	Where I stayed

Sights I took in	Wildlife I saw

Rating	# of days visited
☆☆☆☆☆☆☆☆☆☆	1 2 3 4 5 6 7+

Popular attractions I visited/experienced

☐ Kennecott Copper Mine   ☐ McCarthy River Tours

☐ Root Glacier Trail   ☐

☐ Nabesna Road   ☐

☐ Mount Blackburn   ☐

My Favorite moment

Place for your stamp and overall experience

Yellowstone
NATIONAL PARK

DATE: / /   **FEE:**

☀ ⛅ ☁ 🌦 🌧 ⛈ 🌨 🌨   **TEMP:**

Who was with me	Where I stayed

Sights I took in	Wildlife I saw

Rating	# of days visited
☆☆☆☆☆☆☆☆☆☆	1 2 3 4 5 6 7+

Popular attractions I visited/experienced

☐ Lamar Valley   ☐ Lower Yellowstone River Falls

☐ Grand Canyon of the Yellowstone ☐

☐ Grand Prismatic Spring   ☐

☐ Old Faithful   ☐

My Favorite moment

Place for your stamp and overall experience

Yosemite
NATIONAL PARK

DATE: / / **FEE:**

TEMP:

Who was with me	Where I stayed

Sights I took in	Wildlife I saw

Rating	# of days visited
☆☆☆☆☆☆☆☆☆☆	1 2 3 4 5 6 7+

Popular attractions I visited/experienced

☐ Glacier Point   ☐ Tunnel View

☐ Yosemite Valley   ☐ Tioga Pass

☐ Mariposa Grove of Giant
  Sequoias   ☐

☐ Half Dome   ☐

My Favorite moment

Place for your stamp and overall experience

Zion
NATIONAL PARK

DATE: /   /   FEE:

TEMP:

Who was with me	Where I stayed

Sights I took in	Wildlife I saw

Rating	# of days visited
☆☆☆☆☆☆☆☆☆☆	1 2 3 4 5 6 7+

Popular attractions I visited/experienced

- [ ] The Narrows
- [ ] Angel's Landing
- [ ] Zion Canyon Scenic Drive
- [ ] Zion Shuttle

- [ ] Emerald Pools
- [ ]
- [ ]
- [ ]

My Favorite moment

Place for your stamp and overall experience

NATIONAL PARK

DATE: / /	FEE:

TEMP:

Who was with me	Where I stayed

Sights I took in	Wildlife I saw

Rating	# of days visited
☆☆☆☆☆☆☆☆☆☆	1 2 3 4 5 6 7+

Popular attractions I visited/experienced

☐
☐
☐
☐

☐
☐
☐
☐

My Favorite moment

Place for your stamp and overall experience

NATIONAL PARK

DATE: / /   **FEE:**

TEMP:

Who was with me	Where I stayed

Sights I took in	Wildlife I saw

Rating	# of days visited
☆☆☆☆☆☆☆☆☆☆	1 2 3 4 5 6 7+

Popular attractions I visited/experienced

☐   ☐

☐   ☐

☐   ☐

☐   ☐

My Favorite moment

Place for your stamp and overall experience

NATIONAL PARK

DATE: / /   **FEE:**

TEMP:

Who was with me	Where I stayed

Sights I took in	Wildlife I saw

Rating	# of days visited
☆☆☆☆☆☆☆☆☆☆	1 2 3 4 5 6 7+

Popular attractions I visited/experienced

☐   ☐

☐   ☐

☐   ☐

☐   ☐

My Favorite moment

Place for your stamp and overall experience

NATIONAL PARK

DATE: / /   **FEE:**

TEMP:

Who was with me	Where I stayed

Sights I took in	Wildlife I saw

Rating	# of days visited
☆☆☆☆☆☆☆☆☆☆	1 2 3 4 5 6 7+

Popular attractions I visited/experienced

☐   ☐

☐   ☐

☐   ☐

☐   ☐

My Favorite moment

Place for your stamp and overall experience

NATIONAL PARK

DATE: / /   **FEE:**

TEMP:

Who was with me	Where I stayed

Sights I took in	Wildlife I saw

Rating	# of days visited
☆☆☆☆☆☆☆☆☆☆	1 2 3 4 5 6 7+

Popular attractions I visited/experienced

☐   ☐

☐   ☐

☐   ☐

☐   ☐

My Favorite moment

Place for your stamp and overall experience

Notes

Notes

Notes

Notes

Notes

Notes

Notes

Notes

FUN FACTS ABOUT NATIONAL PARKS

Acadia

Acadia is the oldest park east of the Mississippi River and the first instance where the land was donated to the federal government.

American Samoa

The National Park of American Samoa is the only National Park Service site south of the equator. It covers 13,500 total acres: 9,500 land acres and 4,000 marine acres, which are mostly coral reefs.

Arches

There are more than 2,000 natural sandstone arches inside this national park. Landscape Arch is the largest and longest in North America, stretching 306 feet (that's the length of a football field).

Badlands

The park's name goes back to the Oglala Sioux's ancestors, who called it mako sica, translated as "land bad." French-Canadian fur trappers later built on that title, calling it les mauvaises terres a traverser, or "the badlands to cross."

Big Bend

Historically, people traveled to the Hot Springs Historic District in Big Bend to heal their ailments. Today, visitors can soak in the 105-degree water that gushes from the old foundation of a bathhouse.

Biscayne

Did you know that 95 percent of Biscayne National Park is located underwater? Here, you'll find no fewer than 44 documented shipwrecks, though there are hundreds more yet to be discovered. Some date back to the 1500s, but only six of the wrecks have been mapped for divers to explore.

Black Canyon of the Gunnison

This Colorado national park is called "Black Canyon" for the way the sunlight hits it. Because the canyon walls are 2,722 feet tall in the deepest part, the rays only reach the very bottom for 33 minutes each day.

Bryce Canyon

Bryce Canyon National Park sprouts skinny, totem-shaped hoodoo rock formations, some as tall as a 10-storey building.

Canyonlands

Key scenes from Thelma & Louise were filmed in this national park. Today, a Thelma & Louise half-marathon is run every year through the Canyonlands in honor of the 1991 classic.

Capitol Reef

The rocks in Capitol Reef National Park are up to 270 million years old.

Carlsbad Caverns

Carlsbad Caverns National Park in New Mexico is home to the nation's deepest cave, which is 1,593 feet deep.

Channel Islands

Divers and snorkelers can explore the watery remains of the Winfield Scott shipwreck. Between 1850 and 1900, at least 33 ships were wrecked in the Santa Barbara Channel.

Congaree

For a month in early summer, between the end of May and the start of June, thousands of fireflies simultaneously light up each night at exactly the same time for a magical natural show.

Crater Lake

At 1,932 feet deep, Crater Lake National Park in Oregon is the deepest lake in the U.S.

Cuyahoga Valley

True to its name, the Beaver Marsh wetland in Cuyahoga Valley National Park was created by beavers that moved along remnants of canals.

Death Valley

The world's highest official surface temperature was recorded in 1913 at Death Valley National Park's Furnace Creek Ranch: 134 degrees!

Denali

Beyond mile 15 of the Denali Park Road, vistors need to explore the park by bus, bicycle, or on foot, as private vehicles are not allowed to help reduce traffic and protect the natural resources.

Dry Tortugas

Located 70 miles from Key West in the Gulf of Mexico, Dry Tortugas National Park is a collection of seven tiny islands that can be reached only by boat or plane, making it the country's most remote national park.

Everglades

The Everglades is the only subtropical preserve on the North American continent, sheltering one of the largest stands of pine rockland in the world.

Gates of the Arctic

Located completely above the Arctic Circle. Only 10,518 tourists made the trek to this Alaskan park in 2019—that's less than the number of people that visit the Grand Canyon in a single day.

Gateway Arch

Though it might not look like it, the arch is 630 feet tall and 630 feet wide. Since you're not always looking at the arch straight on, you experience an illusion that it's much taller than it is wide.

Glacier

Glacier National Park boasted 150 glaciers in 1910. Only 25 remain a century on.

Glacier Bay

Glaciers cover over 2,000 square miles of this park, which 250 years ago was a single, large tidewater glacier. The Margerie and Johns Hopkins glacier are two of the most stable, while most glaciers in the park are receding.

Grand Canyon

There is actually a community that lives full-time at the base of the canyon. Within the Havasupai Indian Reservation, Supai Village has a population of 208 and is the most remote settlement in the lower 48. In fact, it's so off the grid that the mail has to be delivered by pack mule.

Grand Teton

The park received its name from early 19th century French trappers, who called the Teton Mountain Range "les trois tetons"--which means "the three breasts" or "the three teats."

Great Basin

This park is home to over 40 known caves. The cave life in the system even expands to a newly discovered species of amphipod (also known as a freshwater shrimp) in Model Cave.

Great Sand Dunes

Over 200 ponderosa pine trees that were historically used for food and medicine by American Indian tribes are protected by the park–the only grove of trees on the National Register of Historic Places.

Great Smoky Mountains

The last elk in North Carolina was slaughtered in the late 1700s; Tennessee's elk population had been decimated by the mid-1800s. Fourteen years ago, 50 elk were reintroduced into Great Smoky Mountains National Park and are flourishing.

Guadalupe Mountains

More than 80 miles of trails will lead you through the woodlands, forests, and sand dunes of this park.

Haleakalā

The 1790 eruption in Haleakala National Park on Maui left an unearthly landscape perfect for the astronauts training for the first moon landing.

Hawai'i Volcanoes

As might be perceived by the parks name, two active volcanoes are within the bounds of this national park, Kilauea being the world's most active. They are safe and accessible to visit if you follow the rules of the park.

Hot Springs

The thermal hot springs waters in this park heat naturally to 143ºF.

Indiana Dunes

Indiana Dunes National Park has more plant and animal species than the entire state of Hawaii.

Isle Royale

Isle Royale National Park is the only national park in the United States that completely closes in the off-season. The park is typically closed November through mid-April due to extreme weather conditions.

Joshua Tree

Some rock formations in Joshua Tree National Park are four times older than dinosaurs.

Katmai

Katmai National Park is home to the largest concentration of brown bears in the world. In fact, more bears than people are estimated to live on the Alaska Peninsula.

Kenai Fjords

Kenai Fjords National Park is named for the numerous fjords carved by glaciers moving down the mountains from the Harding Icefield.

Kings Canyon

Kings Canyon was designated by UNESCO as part of the Sequoia-Kings Canyon Biosphere Reserve.

Kobuk Valley

There are 33 times more caribou than tourists at Kobuk Valley National Park.

Lake Clark

Humans first discovered Lake Clark National Park after the Ice Age, nearly 10,000 years ago!

Lassen Volcanic

Four types of volcanoes—shield, composite, cinder cone, and plug dome—can be found in Lassen Volcanic National Park, where they literally bubble and steam.

Mammoth Cave

Mammoth Cave National Park has the longest cave system on Earth, with more than 400 miles explored.

Mesa Verde

Mesa Verde National Park is also a UNESCO World Heritage site and protects over 5000 archeological sites, the largest archaeological preserve in the U.S.

Mount Rainier

Mount Rainier is the most glaciated peak in the contiguous U.S. with 26 major glaciers.

New River Gorge

-The bridge is 876 feet tall and spans over 3,000 feet in length. This makes it the 2nd largest single span steel arch bridge in the Western Hemisphere.

North Cascades

North Cascades National Park was the inspiration behind two iconic Beat Generation novels

Olympic

Covering nearly one million acres, Olympic National Park provides three distinct ecosystems—glaciated mountains, rugged Pacific coastline, and lush temperate forests.

Petrified Forest

Petrified Forest National Park is the only national park site that contains a segment of the Historic Route 66 alignment.

Pinnacles

The California condors at Pinnacles National Park have a wingspan the length of a compact car.

Redwood

Redwood National Park is home to the world's tallest tree called Hyperion, which earned recognition from the Guinness Book of World Records and remarkably grows on a hill.

Rocky Mountain

The first female nature guides were trained in Rocky Mountain National Park.

Saguaro

Saguaro National Park is the one place in the world you can find the giant 70-foot-tall cactus.

Shenandoah

Shenandoah National Park was built by members of the Civilian Conservation Corps, a government jobs program created during the Great Depression of the 1930s. Workers constructed the rock walls, overlooks, picnic grounds, campgrounds, trails, and the Skyline Drive

Theodore Roosevelt

Theodore Roosevelt first came to the Badlands as a game-hunter, but inspired by the rugged landscape, helped to establish 230 million acres of public lands during his presidency.

Virgin Islands

There is an incredible underwater trail in Virgin Islands National Park

Voyageurs

The rock formations at Voyageurs National Park are half as old as the planet.

White Sands

White Sands National Monument spans more than 176,000 acres of New Mexico desert and contains the largest gypsum dune fields in the world.

Wind Cave

A 100-year-old herd of bison still lives at Wind Cave National Park

Wrangell–St. Elias

Wrangell St.Elias has more dall sheep than anywhere else in North America

Yellowstone

The hot springs at Yellowstone are so acidic, they can dissolve a human body overnight

Yosemite

One of the waterfalls at Yosemite National Park looks like lava

Zion

The park is named after the Hebrew word, "Zion." This word translates as "a place of peace and relaxation."

Made in the USA
Coppell, TX
28 February 2021

51018554R00098